My United States

Mississippi

JENNIFER ZEIGER

Children's Press®
An Imprint of Scholastic Inc.

Content Consultant

James Wolfinger, PhD, Associate Dean and Professor
College of Education, DePaul University, Chicago, Illinois

Library of Congress Cataloging-in-Publication Data
Title: Mississippi / by Jennifer Zeiger.
Description: New York, NY : Scholastic Inc., [2018] | Series: A true book | Includes bibliographical references
  and index.
Identifiers: LCCN 2017036699 | ISBN 9780531231678 (library binding : alk. paper) | ISBN 9780531247181
  (pbk. : alk. paper)
Subjects: LCSH: Mississippi—Juvenile literature.
Classification: LCC F341.3 .Z45 2018 | DDC 976.2—dc23
LC record available at https://lccn.loc.gov/2017036699

Photos ©: cover: John Coletti/AWL Images; back cover bottom: James Kirkikis/Alamy Images; back cover ribbon: AliceLiddelle/Getty Images; 3 bottom: Joseph Sohm/age fotostock; 3 map: Jim McMahon; 4 left: Tier und Naturfotografie/Superstock, Inc.; 4 right: Jupiterimages/Thinkstock; 5 bottom: Brian E Kushner/Shutterstock; 5 top: Greg Jenson/The Clarion-Ledger/USA Today; 7 top: Jim West/The Image Works; 7 center top: age fotostock/Superstock, Inc.; 7 center bottom: Clarence Holmes/age fotostock/Superstock, Inc.; 7 bottom: NaturePL/Superstock, Inc.; 8-9: Anne Power/Dreamstime; 11: Cindy Hopkins/Alamy Images; 12: David R. Frazier/The Image Works; 13: John Cancalosi/Alamy Images; 14: Ilene MacDonald/Alamy Images; 15: David R. Frazier Photolibrary, Inc./Alamy Images; 16-17: Sean Pavone/Shutterstock; 19: ZUMA Press Inc./Alamy Images; 20: Tigatelu/Dreamstime; 22 right: grebeshkovmax-im/Shutterstock; 22 left: Atlaspix/Shutterstock; 23 bottom left: Brian E Kushner/Shutterstock; 23 center left: Ian Macpherson/Alamy Images; 23 top left: JAMES PIERCE/Shutterstock; 23 bottom right: Tier und Naturfotografie/Superstock, Inc.; 23 center right: image-BROKER/Superstock, Inc.; 23 top right: Johannesk/Dreamstime; 24-25: H. Charles McBarron, Jr./The Granger Collection; 27: MPI/Getty Images; 29: MPI/Getty Images; 30 bottom: Atlaspix/Shutterstock; 30 top: MPI/Getty Images; 31 top left: North Wind Picture Archives/Alamy Images; 31 bottom: Julie Dermansky/Corbis/Getty Images; 31 top right: CSU Archive/age fotostock; 32: CSU Archive/age fotostock; 33: 1976 Matt Herron/Take Stock/The Image Works; 34-35: Bettmann/Getty Images; 36: Wesley Hitt/Getty Images; 37: Greg Jenson/The Clarion-Ledger/USA Today; 38: Debra Ferguson/age fotostock; 39 background: Carol M. Highsmith/Buyenlarge/Getty Images; 39 inset: Image Source/iStockphoto; 40 inset: Jupiterimages/Thinkstock; 40 bottom: PepitoPhotos/iStockphoto; 41: Desoto Times Today, Rino Dolbi/AP Images; 42 top left: Science History Images/Alamy Images; 42 top right: Historical/Corbis/Getty Images; 42 bottom left: ullstein bild/Getty Images; 42 center: Hulton Archive/Getty Images; 42 bottom right: STEPHANE DE SAKUTIN/AFP/Getty Images; 43 top left: AF archive/Alamy Images; 43 top right: Michael Ochs Archives/Getty Images; 43 center: Benno Friedman/The LIFE Images Collection/Getty Images; 43 bottom left: John Biever/Sports Illustrated/Getty Images; 43 bottom right: Jason LaVeris/FilmMagic/Getty Images; 44 bottom left: Cipariss/Shutterstock; 44 bottom right: Mopic/Shutterstock; 44 top: NaughtyNut/Shutterstock; 45 top right: David Cook/blueshiftstudios/Alamy Images; 45 top left: Dorothy Alexander/Alamy Images; 45 bottom: MPI/Getty Images. Maps by Map Hero, Inc.

1 2 3 4 5 6 7 8 9 10 R 27 26 25 24 23 22 21 20 19 18

Front cover: A cotton field in Clarksdale

Back cover: Devil's Crossroads

Welcome to Mississippi

Find the Truth!

Everything you are about to read is true *except* for one of the sentences on this page.

Which one is **TRUE**?

T or F Mississippi was one of the original 13 states.

T or F Before becoming a state, Mississippi was controlled by France.

UNITED STATES

Mississippi

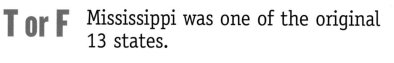

MISSISSIPPI

MSTRMOM

ADAMS

Find the answers in this book.

3

Contents

THE BIG TRUTH!

Mississippi
mud pie

What Represents Mississippi?

Bottlenose
dolphins

4

Mississippi State Fair

Northern mockingbird

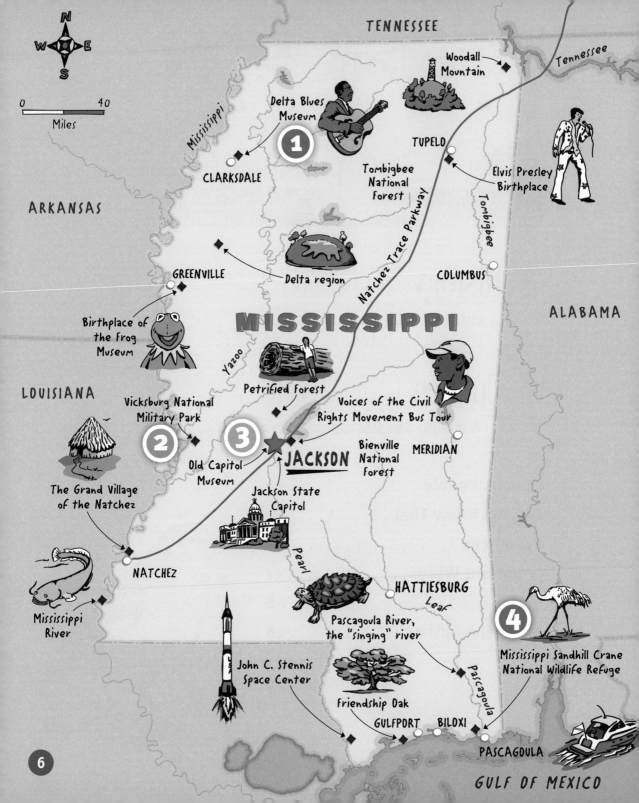

N
W · E
S

0 —— 40
Miles

TENNESSEE

Tennessee

Woodall
Mountain

Delta Blues
Museum
①

CLARKSDALE

Tombigbee
National
Forest

TUPELO

Elvis Presley
Birthplace

ARKANSAS

Tombigbee

Natchez Trace Parkway

GREENVILLE

Delta region

COLUMBUS

Birthplace of
the Frog
Museum

MISSISSIPPI

ALABAMA

Yazoo

Petrified forest

Voices of the Civil
Rights Movement Bus Tour

LOUISIANA

Vicksburg National
Military Park
②

③

Old Capitol
Museum

JACKSON

Bienville
National
Forest

MERIDIAN

The Grand Village
of the Natchez

Jackson State
Capitol

Mississippi
River

NATCHEZ

Pearl

HATTIESBURG

Leaf

Pascagoula River,
the "singing" river

④

Mississippi Sandhill Crane
National Wildlife Refuge

Pascagoula

John C. Stennis
Space Center

Friendship Oak

GULFPORT

BILOXI

PASCAGOULA

GULF OF MEXICO

6

This Is Mississippi!

1 Delta Blues Museum

Mississippi is one of the birthplaces of the musical style known as the blues. Some of the most legendary blues musicians came from Mississippi, including B. B. King and John Lee Hooker.

2 Vicksburg National Military Park

This park and memorial commemorates the people who died during the 47-day **Siege** of Vicksburg during the Civil War (1861–1865).

3 Old Capitol Museum

This is the oldest building in Jackson. Some of Mississippi's most important historical events took place here, including the 1861 vote to leave the United States.

4 Mississippi Sandhill Crane National Wildlife Refuge

Located at the southeastern corner of the state, this coastal landscape was set aside in 1975 to protect the endangered Mississippi sandhill crane.

Native Americans called the Mississippi River *Miss-Sipi* (the great river).

CHAPTER 1

Land and Wildlife

Mississippi is a land of beauty and history. Imagine wandering through dense forests, fishing along the Mississippi River, or taking a dip in the Gulf of Mexico. Everywhere, you'll enjoy the scent of blooming honeysuckle and magnolias. In some parts of the state, you can view a landscape of gently sloping hills. To the south, the coast is lined with beaches, and water stretches beyond the horizon. Welcome to the Magnolia State!

Geography

Mississippi is a place of low **elevation** and many waters. To the northwest is a **fertile** area called the Delta, or Yazoo Basin, which runs along the Mississippi River. East of this area are bluffs and hills. But the hills here are low compared to many other areas of the United States. The highest point is only about 800 feet (244 meters) in elevation. South of the hills are plains and marshes leading down to the Gulf of Mexico.

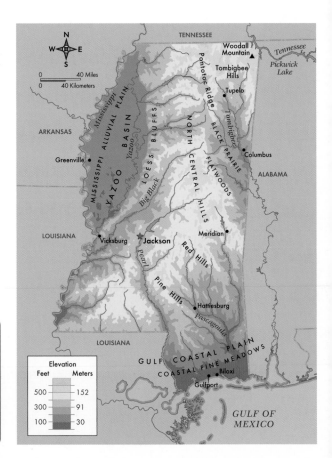

This map shows where the higher (yellow and orange) and lower (green) areas are in Mississippi.

Winterville Mounds

While some of the rolling hills of Mississippi were made by nature, others are human-made. Prehistoric people built huge mounds in western Mississippi near Winterville around the year 1000 CE. These mounds still stand today. The tallest is about the height of a five-story building! The people who built the mounds may have used them for religious ceremonies or other important purposes. Experts believe the mounds were abandoned by 1450. No one is sure why the people left.

A long bridge spans the Mississippi River from Natchez, Mississippi, to Vidalia, Louisiana.

Many Waters

Rivers flow throughout Mississippi. Lakes and ponds dot the landscape. The biggest river is the one that gives the state its name—the Mississippi. Other rivers include the Tombigbee, the Pascagoula, and the Pearl. These waterways feed the fertile forests, marshes, and croplands that cover the state. They also provide plenty of opportunities for recreation, from boating to fishing to swimming.

What's the Weather?

Mississippians often enjoy mild weather. Summers warm up to about 90 degrees Fahrenheit (32 degrees Celsius). Plenty of rain helps crops and wild plants grow. The weather becomes drier and cooler in fall. Winter temperatures usually don't dip below freezing. Sometimes, however, the weather is brutal. Hurricane season lasts from about June through October. During this time, strong storms can blow in from the Atlantic Ocean and damage communities near the Gulf Coast.

MAXIMUM TEMPERATURE
115° F

MINIMUM TEMPERATURE
-19° F

In 2005, Hurricane Katrina caused massive damage along Mississippi's coast.

Huge cypress trees grow in Mississippi's swamps.

Forests and Fields

With more than half of its land covered in forests, Mississippi is alive with plant life. Massive live oaks thrive in the warm, wet south. Beautiful magnolia and oak trees can be seen throughout the state, both in the wild and in parks and yards. Pecan trees are also common. Many flowers bloom in fields and gardens. Scarlet rose mallows, blazing stars, and Carolina lilies are just a few colorful examples.

Creatures Large and Small

Mississippi has a range of wild animals from armadillos and cottontail rabbits to white-tailed deer. There are more deadly creatures, too. Venomous snakes such as cottonmouths slither along the ground. American alligators stalk the swamps.

Birds are a sight to see in Mississippi. The Mississippi Flyway is a major North American bird **migration** route. Hundreds of different species fly through each spring and fall.

Black skimmers are among the many birds that live along Mississippi's Gulf Coast.

Mississippi's current state capitol was built on the site of an old prison.

CHAPTER 2

Government

Jackson's oldest building is the Old State Capitol. Completed in 1839, it saw some major events, including the creation of two state constitutions! In 1903, officials packed up their offices and moved to a brand-new building. This new capitol originally held offices for Mississippi's government. The state supreme court eventually moved to its own building. Still, the "new" capitol remains home to offices for **legislators**, the governor, and other leaders.

Government Branches

Mississippi's state government is divided into three branches. The governor oversees the executive branch, which enforces laws. This branch also includes the lieutenant governor and heads of departments such as health and education. The judicial branch is made up of courts. It interprets the state's laws. The legislative branch writes the state's laws. It includes two houses: the House of Representatives and the Senate.

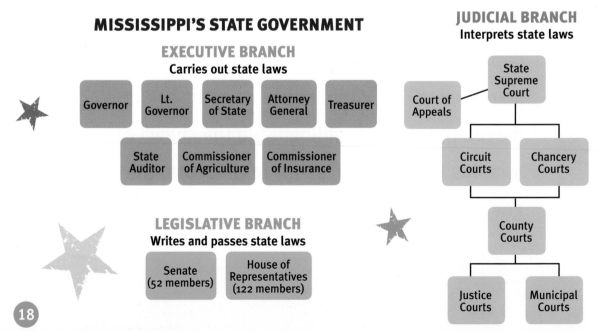

MISSISSIPPI'S STATE GOVERNMENT

EXECUTIVE BRANCH
Carries out state laws

Governor | Lt. Governor | Secretary of State | Attorney General | Treasurer

State Auditor | Commissioner of Agriculture | Commissioner of Insurance

LEGISLATIVE BRANCH
Writes and passes state laws

Senate (52 members) | House of Representatives (122 members)

JUDICIAL BRANCH
Interprets state laws

State Supreme Court

Court of Appeals

Circuit Courts | Chancery Courts

County Courts

Justice Courts | Municipal Courts

Odd Elections

Of the 50 states, 45 of them elect state officials in the same year as national elections. This always happens in an even-numbered year. Mississippi is one of five states that do not hold elections at this time. Instead, voters elect the governor and other

Phil Bryant was elected governor in 2011.

officials in odd-numbered years, one year before the presidential election. For example, while the president and 45 states' governors were elected in 2016, Mississippi elected its governor in 2015.

Mississippi in the National Government

Each state sends elected officials to represent it in the U.S. Congress. Like every state, Mississippi has two senators. The U.S. House of Representatives relies on a state's population to determine its numbers. Mississippi has four representatives in the House.

Every four years, states vote on the next U.S. president. Each state is granted a number of electoral votes based on its number of members in Congress. With two senators and four representatives, Mississippi has six electoral votes.

2 senators and 4 representatives

6 electoral votes

With six electoral votes, Mississippi's voice in presidential elections is about average.

Representing Mississippi

Elected officials in Mississippi represent a population with a range of interests, lifestyles, and backgrounds.

Ethnicity (2015 estimates)

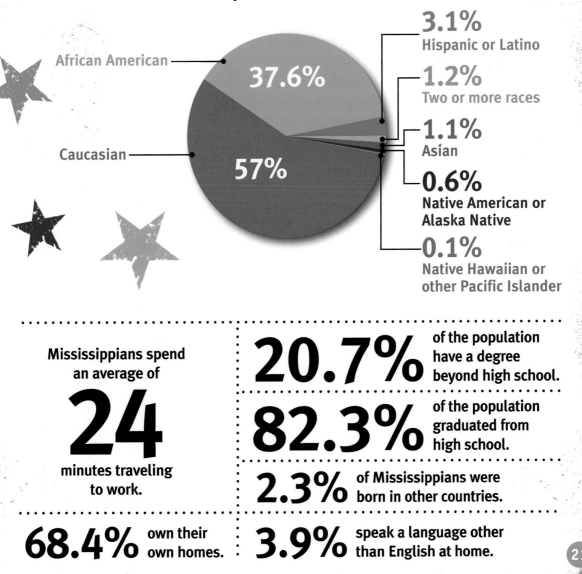

African American — 37.6%

Caucasian — 57%

3.1%
Hispanic or Latino

1.2%
Two or more races

1.1%
Asian

0.6%
Native American or Alaska Native

0.1%
Native Hawaiian or other Pacific Islander

Mississippians spend an average of **24** minutes traveling to work.

68.4% own their own homes.

20.7% of the population have a degree beyond high school.

82.3% of the population graduated from high school.

2.3% of Mississippians were born in other countries.

3.9% speak a language other than English at home.

What Represents Mississippi?

States choose specific animals, plants, and objects to represent the values and characteristics of the land and its people. Find out why these symbols were chosen to represent Mississippi or discover surprising curiosities about them.

Seal

The eagle on the seal holds an olive branch in its right claw. The olive branch stands for peace. In its left claw, the eagle holds arrows. This means the state is also ready for war.

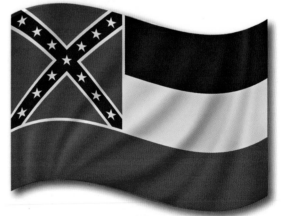

Flag

The Mississippi state flag's red, white, and blue stripes match the national colors of the United States. The design at the top left features the battle flag used by the Confederate states during the Civil War (1861–1865). Though this design once appeared on many other southern state flags, all except Mississippi have removed it.

White-Tailed Deer

STATE LAND MAMMAL
These deer live as far north as Canada and as far south as Peru.

Petrified Wood

STATE STONE
These rocks were once trees. Over millions of years, minerals replaced all parts of the trees.

Honeybee

STATE INSECT
Though this bee is now found around the world, it originally lived only in Africa, the Middle East, and Europe.

Magnolia

STATE FLOWER AND TREE
Unlike many flowers, magnolias are not pollinated by bees. Their main pollinators are beetles.

Northern Mockingbird

STATE BIRD
This mockingbird can imitate not only other birds, but also cats, dogs, and other animals.

Bottlenose Dolphin

STATE WATER MAMMAL
These clever animals sometimes work with other dolphins or even humans to find and capture food.

About 100,000 Mississippians fought in the Civil War (1861-1865).

CHAPTER 3

History

History is alive in Mississippi. Earthen mounds built by prehistoric people are scattered across the state. Plantation buildings from the early 1800s dot the landscape, from large mansions to abandoned slave quarters. The state's more recent past is preserved in **civil rights** memorials and numerous cultural museums. Reminders of Mississippi's fascinating history are present everywhere you may go.

The First in Mississippi

Historians think that Mississippi has been inhabited for about 12,000 years. The first people here were **nomads**. They traveled from place to place, hunting animals and gathering plants for food. Over time, technologies and cultures changed. Many groups began to settle in more permanent communities.

By the 1700s, the three largest groups in what is now Mississippi were the Choctaw, Chickasaw, and Natchez.

This map shows some of the major tribes that lived in what is now Mississippi before Europeans came.

The Choctaw lived in villages in southern and central Mississippi. They were expert farmers and often sold or traded their extra corn, beans, and pumpkins. The Chickasaw shared **ancestors** with the Choctaw but had a separate culture. They lived a more nomadic lifestyle in northeastern Mississippi. Apart from these groups were the Natchez. Their organized villages were scattered across southwestern Mississippi. The Natchez grew crops and created huge earthen mounds on which they built temples.

Outsiders Arrive

The first Europeans in Mississippi arrived in late 1540. Spanish explorer Hernando de Soto was hunting for silver and gold. Finding none in the region, he and his men left. In 1682, Frenchman René Robert Cavelier, sieur de La Salle traveled down the lower Mississippi River. He saw land that was lush with life and a river that could provide access to much of the continent. He knew this was valuable land. He claimed the area, including modern-day Mississippi and Alabama, for France.

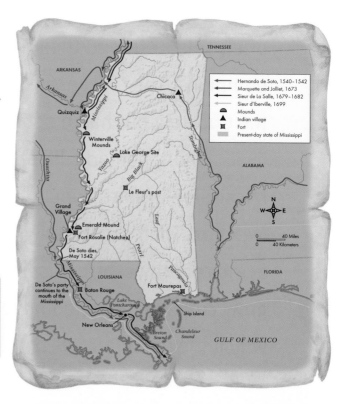

This map shows routes European explorers took as they explored and settled what is now Mississippi.

The French and Indian War helped Great Britain gain control over much of North America.

France's relationship with local Native Americans began peacefully. By 1716, however, they were at war. Within 20 years, the Natchez were largely wiped out. Hundreds of them were forced into slavery. Others joined Chickasaw or other native communities. In 1754, native groups were pulled into both sides of the French and Indian War between France and Great Britain. France lost the war and much of its land, including what is now Mississippi, to the British in 1763.

Becoming Mississippi

In 1798, Mississippi became an American territory. U.S. settlers began pouring in. In 1817, Mississippi became the 20th state. White settlers competed with Native Americans for land. The U.S. government took the side of the white settlers. In the 1830s, it forced the Chickasaw, Choctaw, and other native groups west to Oklahoma.

Timeline of Mississippi Events

December 10, 1817
Mississippi becomes the 20th state.

ca. 10,000 BCE	1540 CE	1817	1830s

ca. 10,000 BCE
The first people arrive in what is now Mississippi.

1540 CE
Hernando de Soto and his men become the first Europeans to visit Mississippi.

1830s
Native Americans are forced out of Mississippi.

Cotton was big business in Mississippi in the early 1800s. Some farmers grew this crop on vast plantations that relied on slave labor. Many Americans, however, spoke against slavery. To keep slavery going, Mississippi and 10 other southern states **seceded** from the country. The United States fought back, kicking off the Civil War in 1861. Four years later, the war ended in defeat for the South. Slavery was **abolished** and the South rejoined the country.

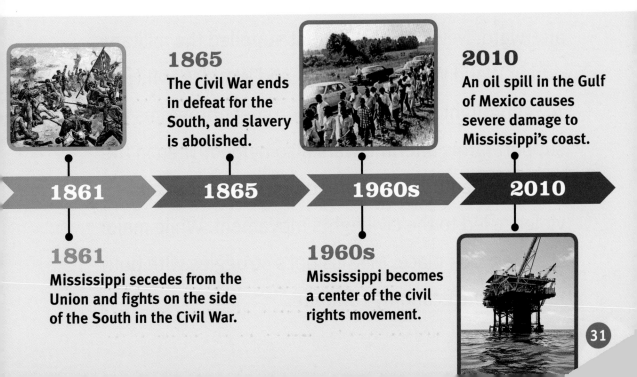

1865
The Civil War ends in defeat for the South, and slavery is abolished.

2010
An oil spill in the Gulf of Mexico causes severe damage to Mississippi's coast.

1861 ▶ 1865 ▶ 1960s ▶ 2010

1861
Mississippi secedes from the Union and fights on the side of the South in the Civil War.

1960s
Mississippi becomes a center of the civil rights movement.

Rebuilding

Much of Mississippi's land had been destroyed during the Civil War, and the state was slow to redevelop afterward. New businesses that supplied the military during World War I (1914–1918) and World War II (1939–1945) brought some relief. Government programs to support farms after the wars also helped. Then in the mid-20th century, widespread **discrimination** and violence led to the civil rights movement. While major changes took place, Mississippi's struggles with both race and the economy continue.

Fannie Lou Hamer

Born in Montgomery County, Fannie Lou Hamer (1917–1977) was a civil rights activist. In 1962, she joined the Student Nonviolent Coordinating Committee (SNCC). Racist laws and government officials tried to prevent black people from voting and exercising other rights in Mississippi. SNCC worked to change that. In 1964, Hamer helped found the Mississippi Freedom Democratic Party (MFDP). The state's existing Democratic Party did not allow people of color to run for office as Democrats. MFDP was created to field black candidates for office in the state.

Throughout her career, Hamer was threatened, arrested, and beaten. But she never stopped. Her efforts live on today as a shining example of the civil rights movement.

Elvis Presley was born in Tupelo.

CHAPTER 4

Culture

The people of Mississippi have a rich cultural heritage, from music and books to sports and food. Look for intricate works of beading and basketry from Choctaw traditions. B. B. King played the blues of the Delta region. Elvis Presley showed people how to shake their hips to rock and roll. And the unforgettable works of such authors as Richard Wright, Tennessee Williams, and William Faulkner are celebrated worldwide.

Two Mississippi State Bulldogs celebrate a win in 2014.

Sports and Recreation

Football is a way of life in Mississippi. People by the thousands cheer on their local college teams. This is particularly true for the Ole Miss Rebels of the University of Mississippi and the Mississippi State Bulldogs. Football greats Archie Manning, Eli Manning, and Brett Favre all played for Mississippi universities.

People in Mississippi also love outdoor activities. Fishing and hunting are popular throughout the state. Boating and camping are common activities, too.

Celebrations

Mississippians know how to celebrate. A variety of festivals offer people a taste of the state's varied culture. Head to the Mississippi Delta Blues & Heritage Festival to get your fill of blues and gospel music. Are you a fan of crawdads? People also call these shellfish "crayfish" or "crawfish." Head to the Country Cajun Crawfish Festival for a bite. There is also the annual state fair in Jackson, which offers a little of everything!

Visitors to the Mississippi State Fair can enjoy food, rides, and more.

Work

Mississippi's economy has long centered on agriculture. A large portion of the state's farming income comes from chickens. Cotton remains an important crop. Catfish are another major product. They are usually raised on fish farms.

Factories, particularly for ships, furniture, and food, provide many jobs. Drilling for oil and natural gas is also a major part of the economy.

Many people work at the John C. Stennis Space Center, where they test rockets for the National Aeronautics and Space Administration (NASA).

Modern farmers use powerful tractors to harvest cotton quickly.

A New Industry

In the 20th century, Mississippi was struggling economically. To bring more money into the state, government leaders looked for ways to make Mississippi less reliant on agriculture. One of the most drastic changes happened in 1990. That year, the government legalized gambling along the Gulf Coast and the Mississippi River. Almost immediately, both jobs and the state income increased. Casinos are now a major part of the state's economy.

Many of Mississippi's casinos are aboard riverboats.

Mississippi Meals

If you're searching for delicious food, look no farther than Mississippi. Barbecues are common when the weather is nice. Enjoy meat cooked in tasty sauces, corn on the cob, hush puppies, okra, and even fried dill pickles. And don't forget a cold glass of sweet tea!

★ ★ Mississippi Mud Pie ★

Ask an adult to help you!

Ingredients

- 1/2 cup butter
- 2 cups graham cracker crumbs
- 1 cup sugar, divided
- 1 package (8 ounces) cream cheese
- 1 container (12 ounces) whipped cream, divided
- 1 package (3.5 ounces) chocolate pudding mix
- 1 package (3.5 ounces) butterscotch pudding mix
- 3 cups milk

Directions

Place the butter in a microwave-safe bowl and warm it in the microwave to melt it. Then mix the melted butter with the graham cracker crumbs and 1/4 cup of the sugar. Press the mixture evenly into the bottom of a pie pan to form the crust. Blend the cream cheese, half of the whipped cream, and the remaining 3/4 cup sugar. Spread this mixture evenly on top of the crust. Combine the pudding mixes and milk and mix well. Spread the mixture evenly on top of the cream cheese mixture. Refrigerate, then add the remaining whipped cream on top.

Small but Important

Mississippi may not be a very large state, but it has played a huge role in America's history. Residents enjoy having natural beauty all around them even when they are close to major cities. People from all over the world have settled in Mississippi, bringing new ideas and energy with them. This remarkable state is sure to remain a great place to live, work, and play for many years to come! ★

Tunica River Park was opened in 2004 as a monument to people who have worked along the Mississippi River throughout history.

Famous People

Elizabeth Lee Hazen

(1885–1975) was a scientist who helped create a lifesaving antifungal medication called nystatin. She was born in the town of Rich.

Tennessee Williams

(1911–1983) was a playwright whose best-known works include *The Glass Menagerie* and *A Streetcar Named Desire*. He was from Columbus.

William Faulkner

(1897–1962) was the Nobel Prize-winning author of novels such as *The Sound and the Fury* and *As I Lay Dying*. He was from New Albany.

Medgar Evers

(1925–1963) was a civil rights activist who was murdered by a white supremacist for his efforts to improve voting rights and end segregation in the South. He was from Decatur.

B. B. King

(1925–2015) was a blues singer and guitarist whose playing has influenced countless other musicians. He was born in Itta Bena.

James Earl Jones

(1931–) is an award-winning actor who has played the voices of Mufasa in *The Lion King* and Darth Vader in the *Star Wars* series. He was born in Arkabutla.

Elvis Presley

(1935–1977) was a world-famous musician and actor. He was nicknamed the King of Rock and Roll. He was from Tupelo.

Jim Henson

(1936–1990) was a puppeteer and filmmaker most famous for creating Kermit the Frog and other Muppet characters. He was from Greenville.

Walter Payton

(1954–1999) was a star running back for the Chicago Bears. He was born in Columbia.

Oprah Winfrey

(1954–) is a TV star and businesswoman who is most famous for hosting *The Oprah Winfrey Show*. She was born in Kosciusko.

Did You Know That ...

Mississippi is a center for soda. Barq's Root Beer was created in Biloxi, and Coca-Cola was first bottled at a candy store in Vicksburg.

A shoe store in Vicksburg was the first in the world to sell shoes as pairs in boxes.

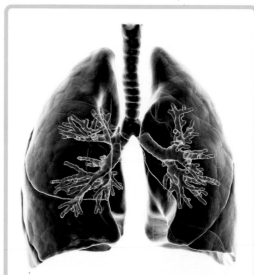

A surgeon with the University of Mississippi performed the world's first human lung transplant in Jackson in 1963.

Many Mississippi artists specialize in creating complex and beautiful quilts.

President Theodore Roosevelt was on a hunting trip in rural Mississippi when he refused to shoot a bear his team had captured. The event inspired toymakers to create a stuffed bear they named Teddy's Bear, after the president.

Did you find the truth?

F Mississippi was one of the original 13 states.

T Before becoming a state, Mississippi was controlled by France.

Resources

Books

Nonfiction

Benoit, Peter. *The Civil War*. New York: Children's Press, 2012.

Dell, Pamela. *Mississippi*. New York: Children's Press, 2014.

Fiction

Taylor, Mildred D. *Mississippi Bridge*. New York: Dial Books for Young Readers, 1990.

Taylor, Mildred D. *Roll of Thunder, Hear My Cry*. New York: Dial Press, 1976.

Wiles, Deborah. *Love, Ruby Lavender*. San Diego: Harcourt, 2003.

Visit this Scholastic website for more information on Mississippi:
★ www.factsfornow.scholastic.com
Enter the keyword **Mississippi**

Important Words

abolished (uh-BAH-lishd) officially ended

ancestors (AN-ses-turz) members of your family who lived long ago

civil rights (SIV-uhl RITEZ) basic rights guaranteed to all citizens, such as the right to vote and the right to equal treatment under the law

discrimination (dis-krim-uh-NAY-shuhn) unfair treatment of others based on differences such as age, race, or gender

elevation (el-uh-VAY-shuhn) a measurement of how high something is above sea level

fertile (FUR-tuhl) good for growing crops and plants

legislators (LEJ-is-lay-turz) elected officials who make or change laws for a country or state

migration (mye-GRAY-shuhn) movement from one area to another

nomads (NOH-madz) members of a community that travels from place to place instead of living in the same place all the time

seceded (suh-SEED-id) formally withdrew from a group or organization

siege (SEEJ) a situation in which a military force blocks its enemy from leaving a certain place or area

Index

Page numbers in **bold** indicate illustrations.

About the Author

Jennifer Zeiger is an editor and author living in Chicago, Illinois. She has written several nonfiction books on a range of topics, from history to science. Her first exposure to Mississippi was through the works of Mississippi author Mildred D. Taylor, which led to a deep and lifelong interest in the region and its history.